TODO ACERCA DEL OTOÑO/ALL ABOUT FALL

Las hojas en otoño/
Leaves in Fall

por/by Martha E. H. Rustad

Traducción/Translation: Dr. Martín Luis Guzmán Ferrer
Editor consultor/Consulting Editor: Dra. Gail Saunders-Smith

Capstone
press

Mankato, Minnesota

Pebble Plus is published by Capstone Press,
151 Good Counsel Drive, P.O. Box 669, Mankato, Minnesota 56002.
www.capstonepress.com

1 2 3 4 5 6 14 13 12 11 10 09

Library of Congress Cataloging-in-Publication Data
Rustad, Martha E. H. (Martha Elizabeth Hillman), 1975–
   [Leaves in fall. Spanish & English]
   Las hojas en otoño = Leaves in fall / por/by Martha E. H. Rustad.
   p. cm. — (Pebble plus. Todo acerca del otoño/All about fall)
   Includes index.
   Summary: "Simple text and photographs present leaves in fall — in both English and Spanish" —
Provided by publisher.
   ISBN-13: 978-1-4296-3260-7 (hardcover)
   ISBN-10: 1-4296-3260-7 (hardcover)
   1. Leaves — Juvenile literature. 2. Fall foliage — Juvenile literature. I. Title. II. Title: Leaves in fall.
QK649.R8818 2009
578.4'3 — dc22   2008034506

Editorial Credits
Sarah L. Schuette, editor; Katy Kudela, bilingual editor; Adalín Torres-Zayas, Spanish copy editor;
   Veronica Bianchini, designer

Photo Credits
Capstone Press/Karon Dubke, all

Pebble Plus thanks the Minnesota Landscape Arboretum in Chaska, Minnesota, for the use of their
   location during photo shoots.

Note to Parents and Teachers

The Todo acerca del otoño/All about Fall set supports national science standards related
to changes during the seasons. This book describes and illustrates leaves in fall in both
English and Spanish. The images support early readers in understanding the text. The
repetition of words and phrases helps early readers learn new words. This book also
introduces early readers to subject-specific vocabulary words, which are defined in the
Glossary section. Early readers may need assistance to read some words and to use the
Table of Contents, Glossary, Internet Sites, and Index sections of the book.

Table of Contents

Tabla de contenidos

Fall Is Here

Summer is over.
It's fall. Leaves start
to change color.

Llegó el otoño

Ya terminó el verano.
Es otoño. Las hojas
empiezan a cambiar
de color.

4

Colorful Trees

Broad maple leaves
become red, orange,
and yellow.

Árboles de colores

Las anchas hojas del
arce se vuelven rojas,
anaranjadas y amarillas.

6

Oak leaves turn
red and brown.

Las hojas del roble
se tornan rojas
y marrones.

8

Round gingko leaves
change to yellow.

Las hojas redondas
del gingko cambian
a amarillo.

10

Evergreen needles do not change color. They stay green all year.

Las agujas de los árboles perennes no cambian de color. Todo el año están verdes.

Falling Leaves

The weather gets colder.

The days are shorter.

Leaves turn brown and die.

Las hojas que caen

El tiempo se vuelve más frío.

Los días son más cortos.

Las hojas se ponen

marrones y mueren.

14

Leaves float to the
ground. They crunch
under your feet.

Las hojas flotan hacia
el suelo. Crujen bajo
tus pies.

16

17

People rake leaves
in fall. You can
play in the piles.

Las personas rastrillan
las hojas del suelo.
Tú puedes jugar en
los montoncitos.

A New Season

The trees are bare.

Winter is here.

A new season begins.

Una nueva estación

Los árboles están desnudos.

Llegó el invierno. La nueva

estación ha empezado.

20

Glossary

bare — not covered or empty; trees look bare when the leaves fall off.

broad — wide; maple leaves are broad with pointed edges.

crunch — to make a loud noise when crushed

evergreen — a tree that has green leaves all year

needle — a thin, pointed leaf on an evergreen tree

season — one of the four parts of the year; the seasons are spring, summer, fall, and winter.

Glosario

aguja — la hoja delgada y puntiaguda de los árboles perennes

ancho — amplio; las hojas del arce son anchas y con los bordes en punta.

crujiente — que hace un ruido fuerte cuando lo aplastas

desnudo — no cubierto o vacío; los árboles se ven desnudos cuando se les caen las hojas.

la estación — una de las cuatro partes del año; las estaciones son primavera, verano, otoño e invierno.

perennes — árboles que tienen hojas todo el año

Internet Sites

FactHound offers a safe, fun way to find educator-approved Internet sites related to this book.

Here's what you do:

1. Visit *www.facthound.com*
2. Choose your grade level.
3. Begin your search.

This book's ID number is 9781429632607.

FactHound will fetch the best sites for you!

Index

Sitios de Internet

FactHound te brinda una forma segura y divertida de encontrar sitios de Internet relacionados con este libro y aprobados por docentes.

Lo haces así:

1. Visita *www.facthound.com*
2. Selecciona tu grado escolar.
3. Comienza tu búsqueda.

El número de identificación de este libro es 9781429632607.

¡FactHound buscará los mejores sitios para ti!

Índice